Rubbish & Recycling

Stephanie Turnbull

Designed by Andrea Slane and Michelle Lawrence

Illustrated by Christyan Fox

Rubbish and recycling consultant: Cecilia Davey, The Young People's
Trust for the Environment and Nature Conservation

Reading consultant: Alison Kelly

Contents

In the bin

Every day people throw away things that are empty, broken, used or just not wanted any more.

The amount of rubbish which is thrown away grows and grows.

Each person throws away about seven times their weight in rubbish every year.

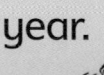

A load of rubbish

Rubbish comes from many places.

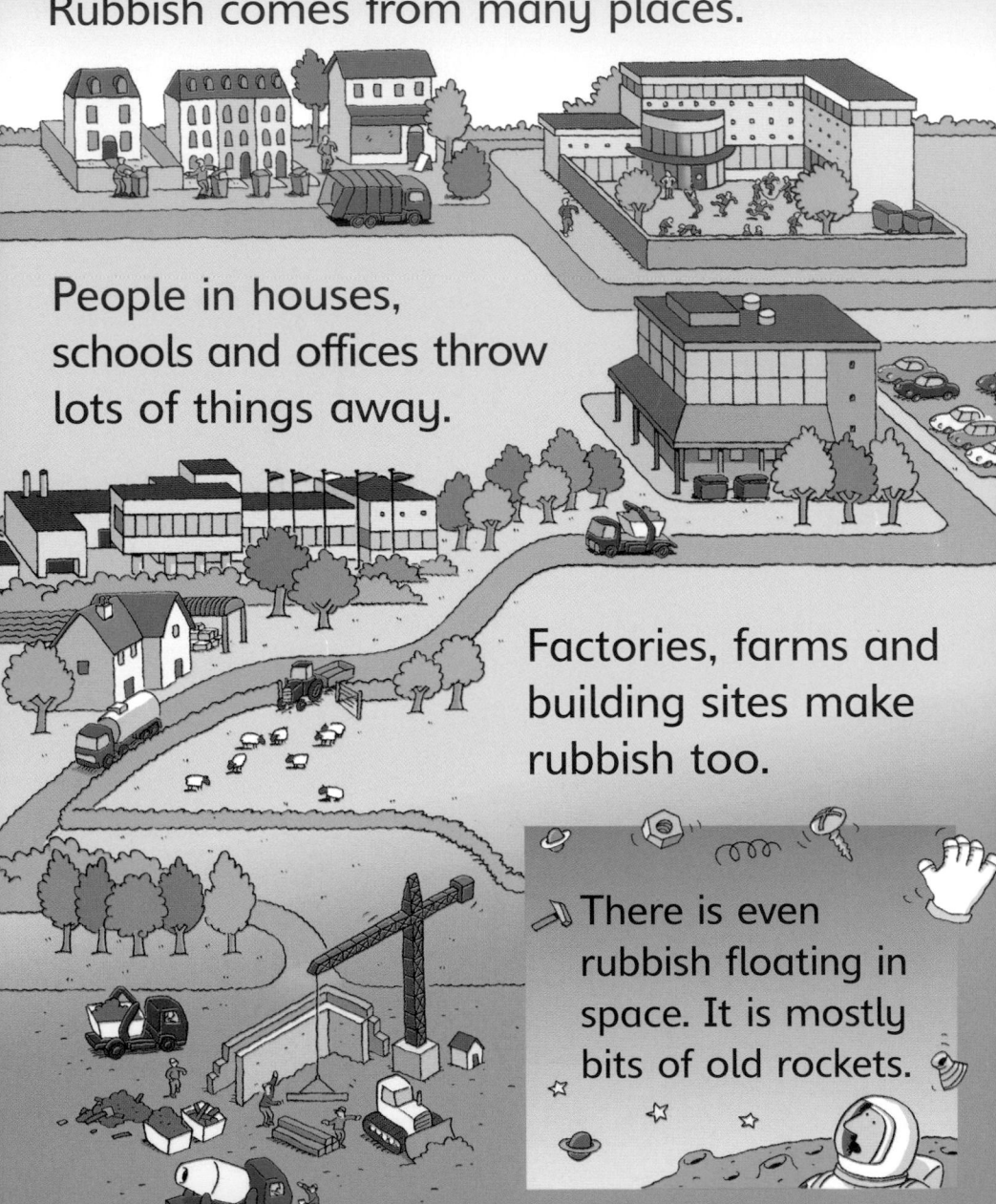

People in houses, schools and offices throw lots of things away.

Factories, farms and building sites make rubbish too.

There is even rubbish floating in space. It is mostly bits of old rockets.

4

Most rubbish is thrown into bins, but sometimes it is dropped on the ground or dumped in rivers and seas.

Dumped rubbish can spread disease and cut or poison wild animals.

Collection time

Trucks come to take away rubbish that has been left out in bins and bags.

This truck has a special lift that picks up big bins and empties them into the truck.

Panel inside the truck

Shovel

1. A shovel scoops rubbish in and packs it against a panel.

2. As the truck fills, the panel slides back to make more room.

3. More rubbish is added and is squashed up inside the truck.

The city of Venice, in Italy, has canals instead of streets so its rubbish is collected in boats.

On the move

When rubbish has been collected, it is taken to a place called a transfer station.

Trucks tip their loads of rubbish down a deep chute at the transfer station.

A heavy metal ram pushes the rubbish into enormous metal boxes.

Long, flat trucks carry the boxes to places where the rubbish will be buried or burned.

At some transfer
stations, boxes are
loaded onto ships or
trains instead of trucks.

Some trains can carry more than
200 boxes of rubbish.

9

Buried deep

The boxes of rubbish are emptied out at a place called a landfill.

The rubbish is spread out and squashed by a compactor truck.

1. The compactor's wide, spiked wheels flatten the rubbish.

2. Diggers spread soil over the top of the rubbish.

3. The next day, new boxes of rubbish are added to the landfill.

4. The landfill grows bit by bit until it looks like a hill.

Full landfills are covered with grass. Soon there won't be enough land left to build new ones.

Up in flames

Some rubbish doesn't go to landfills.
Instead it is burned in an incinerator.

1. Trucks tip rubbish
into a deep pit at
the incinerator.

2. A grabber picks up
the rubbish and feeds
it into a huge fire.

3. Ash from the fire
is put in a truck and
taken to a landfill.

4. Smoke from the
fire goes out of a
tall chimney.

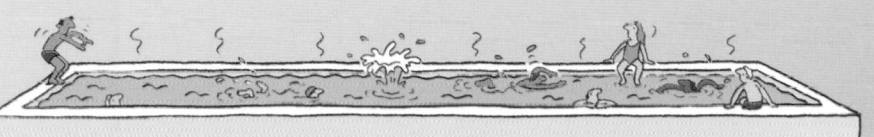

Hot air from incinerators can be used
to heat homes and swimming pools.

This worker at an incinerator is checking
the fire where rubbish is burned. His face
is covered to protect it from the heat.

Dangerous waste

Some rubbish, such as chemicals and engine oil, can harm people, animals and the land.

This man is carrying a tub that contains dangerous chemicals.

The tub is sealed tightly and will be buried in a special landfill.

This is a landfill where chemicals have been buried. They are covered with a special white powder that seals them underground.

Some chemicals are burned in incinerators instead of being buried.

Spilled oil can poison water, so it must be cleaned up quickly.

Down the drain

Every time you have a bath or flush the toilet, the waste water flows away down underground pipes called sewers.

This photograph shows a robot about the size of a basketball. It moves through sewers to check for leaks inside the pipes.

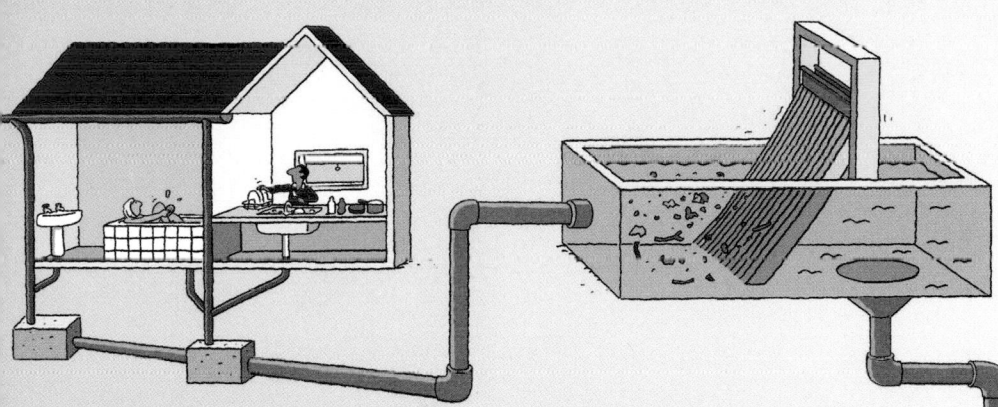

1. Sewers take waste, also called sewage, to a sewage works.

2. A screen traps big pieces of rubbish like rags and sticks.

4. The water is cleaned in other tanks then flows into lakes.

3. The sewage goes into tanks where solid waste sinks.

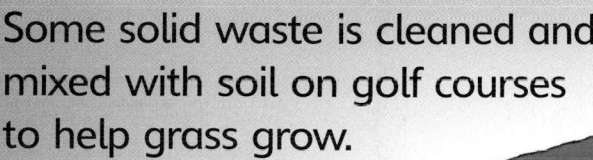

Some solid waste is cleaned and mixed with soil on golf courses to help grass grow.

Recycling

Some rubbish can be made into new things and used again. This is called recycling.

Paper, cardboard, glass, metal and plastic can all be recycled.

In some places there are collection trucks which pick up rubbish that can be recycled.

In other places, people take their cans, bottles and paper to big recycling bins.

The collected rubbish is sorted in factories. These men are checking cans and taking out anything that isn't metal.

There is often a symbol like this on things that can be recycled.

Melting metal

All kinds of metal can be melted down and used again. These pictures show how aluminium drink cans are recycled.

1. Cans are crushed into blocks, then a machine shreds them.

2. Hot air burns any patterns or logos off the bits of metal.

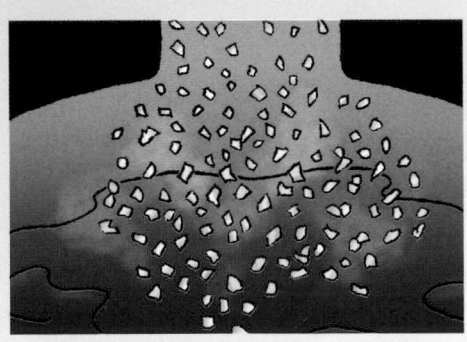

3. Next, the bits of metal are heated until they melt.

4. The melted metal is poured into moulds and left to cool.

Some metal cans are recycled into car or plane parts.

The metal hardens into blocks like these. Each block can be made into more than one million new cans.

Crushed glass

Used glass bottles and jars can be recycled again and again.

1. Old glass is tipped onto a moving belt at a recycling centre.

2. Workers sort the glass and take out big pieces of rubbish.

3. Heavy rollers crush the glass into small pieces.

4. A vacuum sucks up any bits of metal or scraps of paper.

Crushed glass is melted and shaped into new containers, ready to be filled again.

Old glass bottles can be crushed and mixed with gravel to make roads.

Piles of paper

When paper is recycled, it is mixed with water until it is a soggy mush. The mush then goes through different stages.

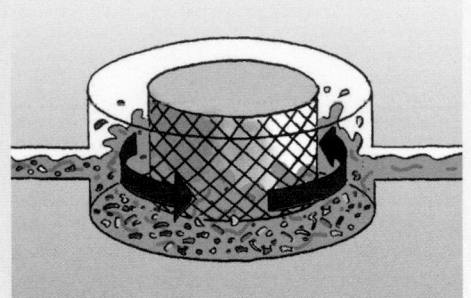

1. It is spun around. Staples and other bits fall to the bottom.

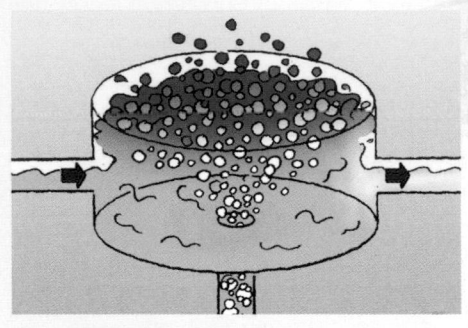

2. Next, soap cleans the mush and gets rid of ink and glue.

3. The mush is then sprayed out onto a moving wire screen.

4. It is squeezed by rollers, dried and wound into a big roll.

Recycled paper is made into
all sorts of things. Here it has been
turned into bedding for cows.

Paper can be recycled several times. Each
time it could become a different product.

One giant roll of recycled paper
can make 80,000 toilet rolls.

Fantastic plastic

Used plastic bottles can be recycled into soft, fleecy material for making clothes. These pictures show how it is done.

1. First, old plastic bottles are collected and sorted by colour.

2. Next, the bottles are cleaned with strong jets of water.

3. Then the bottles are torn into bits by metal rollers.

4. The bits of plastic are melted into a sticky mess.

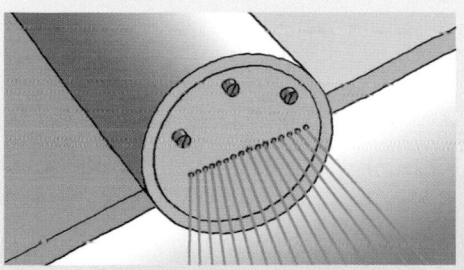

5. Melted plastic is pushed through holes to make long strands.

6. When the strands cool, they are woven into thick material.

This material is often used to make warm fleeces, like the one this climber is wearing.

Plastic bottles that aren't recycled take 800 years to rot away in a landfill.

Rotting away

Some rubbish, such as leaves and vegetable peelings, can be recycled into dark, thick soil called compost.

This machine chops up natural waste from people's gardens. The waste will rot and turn into compost.

Some people have composting bins for all their fruit and vegetable waste.

The waste rots inside the bin. After a few weeks, it has turned into compost.

The compost can then be taken out and put on plants to help them grow.

Worms can be put in composting bins to eat waste and help to turn it into compost.

Glossary

Here are some of the words in this book you might not know. This page tells you what they mean.

 transfer station - a place where trucks take rubbish to be packed into boxes.

 landfill - an area of land that is filled with rubbish and covered with soil.

 compactor - a machine that spreads and flattens rubbish at a landfill.

 incinerator - a building where rubbish is taken to be burned.

 sewage works - a place where waste water is taken to be cleaned.

 aluminium - a silvery metal that is often used to make drink cans.

 compost - a crumbly soil made from rotted fruit, vegetables and other waste.

Websites to visit

You can visit websites to find out more about rubbish and recycling. For links to sites with video clips and activities, go to the Usborne Quicklinks website at **www.usborne.com/quicklinks** and type in the keywords "**beginners rubbish**".

Always ask an adult before using the internet and make sure you follow these basic rules:

1. Never give out personal information, such as your name, address, school or telephone number.

2. If a website asks you to type in your name or email address, check with an adult first.

The websites are regularly reviewed and the links at Usborne Quicklinks are updated. However, Usborne Publishing is not responsible and does not accept liability for the content or availability of any website other than its own. We recommend that children are supervised while on the internet.

Garden waste is often loaded onto a truck from bins like these, and then taken away for recycling.

Index

Acknowledgements

Photographic manipulation by Nick Wakeford, John Russell and Mike Wheatley

Photo credits

The publishers are grateful to the following for permission to reproduce material:

Cover © Alamy/David Hoffman; **p1** © Alamy/Jon Banfield; **p2-3** © Creatas; **p5** © Nature Picture Library/Michael Durham; **p9** © Alamy/Justin Case; **p10** © Zefa/Claudius; **p13** © keithwoodphotography.com; **p14** © TEK Image/Science Photo Library; **p15** © Robert Brook/Science Photo Library; **p16** © Peter Menzel/Science Photo Library; **p19** © Alamy/Jeff Morgan; **p21** © Novelis Recycling; **p23** © Rockware Glass; **p25** © Phil Matt/Agstock/Science Photo Library; **p27** © Alamy/John Foxx; **p28-29** © Viridor Waste Management; **p31** © Alamy/Jeff Morgan.

Sun, moon and stars

Farm animals

Elizabeth I

Rubbish & Recycling

Dogs

Horses and ponies

Spiders

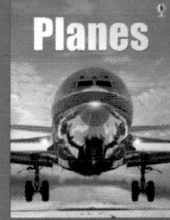
Planes

Cats

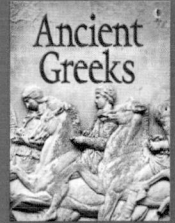
Ancient Greeks

VOLCANOES

DINOSAURS

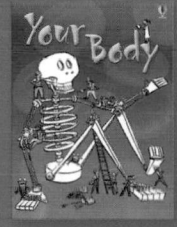
Your Body

Armour

Sharks

The Celts

VIKINGS

Castles

How flowers grow

Digging up the past

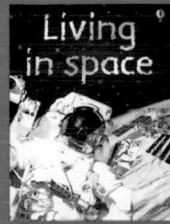
Living in space

Caterpillars and Butterflies

Ballet

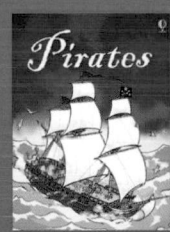
Pirates

EGYPTIANS

Eggs and Chicks

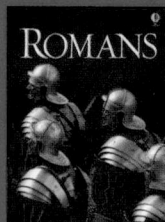
ROMANS

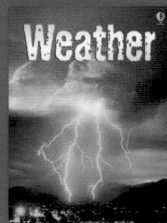
Weather

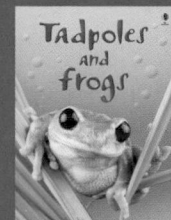
Tadpoles and frogs

Why do we eat?

Under the sea

Bears

AZTECS

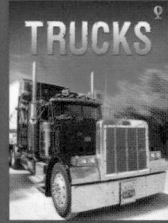
TRUCKS

Night Animals

Firefighters

Antarctica

Bugs

COWBOYS

Planet Earth

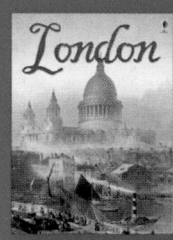
London

Seashore

China

Dangerous Animals

Rainforests

Trees

Reptiles

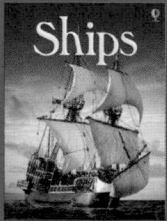
Ships

Bats

Penguins